Take Charge of Your Email Inbox

BONNIE HILLMAN SHAY

iUniverse LLC
Bloomington

TAKE CHARGE OF YOUR EMAIL INBOX

iUniverse books may be ordered through booksellers or by contacting:

iUniverse LLC
1663 Liberty Drive
Bloomington, IN 47403
www.iuniverse.com
1-800-Authors (1-800-288-4677)

Because of the dynamic nature of the Internet, any web addresses or links contained in this book may have changed since publication and may no longer be valid. The views expressed in this work are solely those of the author and do not necessarily reflect the views of the publisher, and the publisher hereby disclaims any responsibility for them.

Any people depicted in stock imagery provided by Thinkstock are models, and such images are being used for illustrative purposes only. Certain stock imagery © Thinkstock.

ISBN: 978-1-4917-3173-4 (sc)
ISBN: 978-1-4917-3174-1 (e)

Library of Congress Control Number: 2014906740

Printed in the United States of America.

iUniverse rev. date: 04/24/2014

CONTENTS

—— LIST OF FIGURES ——

INTRODUCTION

Hi Bonnie,

I just wanted to say a big "thank-you" for your very helpful tips on eliminating and cleaning up my emails in my inbox.

OMG girl—you would not believe what I've been finding. As an example, I searched my inbox for all the "groupon" emails in there. Guess how many were sitting in my inbox—mostly unread—1197—again, OMG. Boy, did I take the time to delete all of those emails—I never realized I was getting 2 and 3 "groupon" emails a day for years! But, no more, and I will "unsubscribe" from them.

So I thank you and my computer thanks you! Wonder what else is cluttering up "my space"??

Cathy C.

Email has become a full-time challenge to manage, both personally and professionally. People have become inundated with the quantity of emails that find their way into their inboxes, and before they know it, 3,000 emails have taken up residence there. As a result, they become overwhelmed, stuck, and don't know what to do. Are <u>you</u> one of these people?

How would you feel . . .

- If your inbox had less than one screen's worth of email in it?
- If you could find any email you were looking for in a few seconds?
- If you didn't miss important items because they weren't buried in your inbox with 2,999 other emails?
- If you felt peaceful and calm because you had regained control of your email?

This is all possible. Although this book is non-fiction, it can become <u>your</u> reality. In the pages ahead, I will share with you how we all got into an email mess and, most importantly, how to get out of it. And if you have been unsuccessful in regaining control of your inbox with other methods or systems, chapter 2—where I prompt you to create your personal vision of how you will feel when you regain control of your inbox—will make the difference for you this time around.

So fasten your seat belts, ladies and gentlemen, and get ready for take-off.

CHAPTER ONE

How We All Got to Having Unmanageable Email Inboxes

Real-Life Example

Susan is fifty-three years old, she works part-time as an accountant, is married, has three children, and has been using email for sixteen years. She has four different email addresses (one personal, one professional, one for junk mail, and one for a not-for-profit board she is on) and receives an average of sixty-five emails a day. She often spends her evenings after dinner catching up on email while her kids are doing homework and she frequently checks email on her phone for a few minutes here and there while waiting to pick her kids up after activities or while cooking dinner. With all that she juggles, she aims to stay informed of discounts on purchases and travel, on the accounting industry, and on some health matters for her daughter. She always feels like she is playing catch up and never on top of her email inbox. Email started out reasonably way back when, but Susan now feels like it is a full-time job and she needs to regain control of it.

You didn't get into a state of email overwhelm overnight; none of us did. It has been an accumulation of many factors and it's worth looking at those factors because if you are aware of how you got here, you are likely to better figure out how to overcome these challenges.

Our inboxes are being swamped by the quantity of emails we receive.

Here are some email stats according to The Radicati Group, Inc., a technology market-research firm (http://www. radicati.com/wp/wp-content/uploads/2010/04/Email-Statistics-Report-2010-2014-Executive-Summary2.pdf).

	2010	2011	2012	2013	2014*
Ave. # of emails sent/received per user per day	74	75	77	79	80
Ave. # of legitimate emails	61	62	63	65	65
Ave. # of spam emails	13	13	14	14	15

*projected

It is amazingly clear that each of us is outnumbered by our emails. There is only one of each of us and there are hundreds of emails coming at us fast and furiously.

We fear deleting something because we think we might need it someday.

We hang on to so much stuff because we want to save it "just in case we need it someday!" On top of that, we rarely go back to review what we have saved and purge what we end up not really needing, so the clutter grows and grows and grows.

We fear missing out on something good.

We have been trained to watch out for every sale, discount, and piece of information that we might "need" someday, and now there are so many people (myself included) who end up spending so much time clipping coupons and saving special offers that it becomes a part-time job just to manage the paper clutter and expiration dates. I truly believe that we waste more time and money by clipping coupons and saving special offers than can ever be truly saved with those coupons and specials. It's a marketing racket that distracts us from more important efforts in our lives. Okay, I'll step down from my soapbox now.

We don't make decisions or we don't make good decisions.

An overflowing inbox is actually **a pile of decisions not made**. In order to stay on top of the volume of emails coming our way, we need to develop better decision-making methods.

We have multiple email addresses and multiple devices to manage.

On average, Americans have three email addresses, according to a Microsoft survey http://www.microsoft.com/en-us/news/features/2011/apr01/04-05hotmailhelps.aspx.

A layer of complexity that many of us deal with is having multiple email addresses: often one address for personal use, another for professional use, and a third for junk mail. Then add in the fact that many of us access our email from our computers, smartphones, and tablets, and you can see that we have created a whole other layer of email-management complexity.

We are surrounded by noise and distractions.

Think of all of the modes of communication that demand our attention all day long: emails, text messages, voicemails, phone calls, TV, telephone, and faxes, not to mention regular postal service mail. (I think someone will bring back smoke signals to get our attention one of these days because that is about the only line of communication not currently being used—that and the carrier pigeon.)

People have more data than ever to process—whether they ask for it or not. Information overload cost American businesses just under $1 trillion in employee time lost to needless emails and other distractions in 2010, according to Jonathan Spira, chief analyst of the New York research firm Basex. The Denver Post.

(http://www.denverpost.com/business/ci_24804417/
employers-step-prevent-worker-burnout#ixzz2osaUrajI.)

According to McKinsey Global Institute, we spend thirteen hours each week dealing with email. That's thirteen hours—28 percent of our workweek—the average person dedicates reading, deleting, sorting, and sending emails (http://www.mckinsey.com/insights/ high_tech_telecoms_internet/the_social_economy).

All of these factors add up to one challenging email mess, but don't give up. Read on to learn how to untangle yourself from your email mess and regain control of your email inbox, thus restoring peace and calm to your life.

CHAPTER TWO

Why Do You Want to Improve Your Email Management?: Your Personal Vision

Real-Life Example

Jon, a successful entrepreneur, was totally overwhelmed with his email inbox. He had this lingering fear of missing an important client deadline because his email was totally out of control, so he constantly felt distracted and anxious. Before Jon and I worked together, I asked him what his vision was for his email inbox.

Here's what he said he wanted:

- Peace of mind in knowing that he could always see the most important emails on his screen.

- To be able to compartmentalize his email efforts so that they didn't interfere with his focus on client work.
- Confidence in knowing where to file emails he needed to save and knowing where to find them when he needed them.
- To eliminate the huge volume of clutter that was filling up his inbox.

By the time we finished working together, Jon had achieved his vision. I've stayed in touch with Jon since then and he is thrilled that he has kept up his email-management habits, which have kept him in control and feeling great about his email management. He is now able to focus on what really matters to him.

I expect that you are reading this book because you personally suffer from email inbox challenges. Maybe you've tried a variety of methods to manage your email, but they haven't worked. Why is that?

All of my life (even before becoming a Professional Organizer), I have heard people say:

- "I wish I was more organized?"
- "Why am I so disorganized?"
- "If only I was more organized, I could do so much more."

And I venture to guess that you've often heard (or said) this favorite new year's resolution: "I'm going to get more organized this year." People who say this have great intentions and they might actually go and buy a new filing cabinet, a new organizing system, or a new software program, but they typically don't make lasting progress toward getting more organized.

Why is this so? Well, saying "I want to get organized" is not a very motivating statement—it doesn't really tell you what it would feel like or what the rewards would be if you did get organized. In order to make substantive change (i.e., transformation), you need an emotional connection to the results of being organized.

I believe that my approach will help you achieve success this time around (no matter how many other methods you may have already tried) because we are going to dig a little deeper and get to <u>WHY</u> you want to be more organized. When you explore what being more organized would allow you to do, you will get to your motivating factors, tangible concepts that you can grab on to. Identifying the emotional charge behind what you are trying to achieve will get you moving toward the goal of being more organized.

Since we are focusing on getting your email inbox de-cluttered and organized, take a few minutes to complete the following exercise before reading the "how to" section of this book. The exercise will help you figure out what your own motivating factors are.

ACTION ITEM: Answer these few questions to unearth your motivating factors.

Why do you want to get your email inbox under control?

_____

_____

_____

_____

What will you be able to do when you have a de-cluttered email inbox solve?

_____

_____

_____

_____

How will you feel with an un-cluttered inbox?

_____

_____

_____

_____

Now that you've got a sense of why you want an un-cluttered inbox (i.e., what motivates you toward this goal), consider how that motivation can be made manifest through a personal vision. Your personal vision should articulate how you expect to feel when your inbox is de-cluttered and the benefits you will achieve. Those benefits may be greater confidence, peace of mind, or focus, more time with your family, less stress, etc.

By spending time imagining what the desired outcome(s) will be like and the benefits and rewards you will experience—to the point that you can almost taste it— you will be motivated to implement the system I lay out in this book.

Here are some sample situations and visions to give you some ideas on how to proceed.

Situation: You get a stomach ache every time you open your inbox because there are 3,000 emails there and you are totally overwhelmed, so you just give up any hope of regaining control.

> **Vision**: I want to have no more than one screen's worth of email so I can see everything at a glance. I won't be overwhelmed, I'll be more confident, less worried, and as a result, more productive.

Situation: You missed an important client email or deadline which was embarrassing and reflected poorly on your client service.

Vision: I want to know where all of my important client emails are so I won't worry about missing deadlines. As a result, I will have greater confidence in my customer service.

ACTION ITEM: Articulate your vision. Imagine what your life would be like if you got your email inbox under control.

_____

_____

_____

_____

Keep in mind that being organized is a MEANS TO AN END, not an end in and of itself. That is a key distinction to make. Think of what you really want to achieve and then realize that being more organized will help you get there. You can do it!

CHAPTER THREE

Our Goals and Our Guiding Principles

Our Goals

This book focuses on one main goal: to de-clutter your email inbox so that it only contains important emails that you need to see and respond to. In order to get there, you need to employ good decision-making skills every step of the way, skills that you will learn in this book.

A secondary, more quantitative goal is to only have one screen's worth of email in your inbox so you don't have to scroll up and down to look at your email. You want to be able to see everything at a glance. Wouldn't that be nice?

Our Guiding Principles

I also want to introduce two guiding principles to help you make the best choices going forward. These principles are universal and can apply to your email inbox and beyond.

First of all, "be proactive, not reactive."

In our fast-paced world, we often fall into the trap of living reactively. The amount of information and stuff coming into our lives bombards our sensibilities. As a result, we lose track of our goals and our priorities, and we are doing things that satisfy other people's agendas, not our own.

For instance, think of all of the messages we get bombarded with in a day via email, snail mail, voicemail, bill boards, TV commercials, etc. Consider identifying your critical path in life (i.e., what you want to do) and filtering out all of the messages that don't support and promote that critical path. Like every time you get mail from a cable TV company promising you that they will lower your cable TV rates. Instead of paying attention to the offer, throw it out (and apply that same rule to the other umpteen solicitations you get in the mail). When you are ready to see if you can lower your bill (or to apply for a credit card, or buy new car insurance), you will do the necessary shopping and comparing and make a choice when you say so, not when the cable TV or credit card company tells you to.

Being more proactive will allow you to:

- stay in control of your time;
- stay on track for your goals/priorities; and
- make more thoughtful decisions.

You'll see lots of examples on how to be proactive throughout this book.

Secondly, "focus on quality, not quantity."

We live in a time in which we have endless choices and endless opportunities to acquire more stuff in our lives. But the more we have, the more there is to manage and the more time that is required of us. I find that the less we have, the more easily we see what really matters, and, of course, the easier it is to manage. Less is more, so put limits on what you keep. The decision-making guidelines included in this book will help you be more discerning on what to keep and how to focus on quality.

NOT ALL EMAILS ARE CREATED EQUAL.

CHAPTER FOUR

Five Steps to De-cluttering Your Email Inbox

1. Unsubscribe
2. Divert (create rule/alert to route to a folder)
3. Delete
4. File
5. Act

Not all emails are created equal, so the following five steps will help you decide what to do with each email. By implementing the following five steps, you will be amazed at the progress you will achieve. You will initially apply the steps to your overflowing inbox and then you will continue to apply them on a daily basis to maintain your new and improved inbox state of being.

To help you visualize the big picture of what you will be doing, I've included flow charts for de-cluttering your email inbox. (See page 38.)

ACTION ITEM:

How many emails are in your inbox right now (before applying any of the five steps)? _____

1. Unsubscribe

Just like all of the junk mail that comes in our snail-mail box, we get a lot of junk mail in our email inboxes. We think we have to deal with this junk mail because it is there, but that is not the case.

Stop the email before it even arrives in your inbox. Don't even let it get in the doorway and take up valuable real estate.

Once upon a time, you subscribed to various newsletters, weekly store ads, and other emails that you thought were relevant, but are now of little or no importance and are cluttering up your inbox. Take ten seconds now to unsubscribe and stem the flow of unimportant emails.

Why should you unsubscribe? Let me count the ways.

- to avoid information overload;
- to minimize distractions;
- to ignore irrelevant material;
- to focus on "quality, not quantity"; and
- to save time by searching for the information you need when you need it, rather than being constantly inundated with mostly irrelevant emails.

How to unsubscribe

- Most newsletters have a "Safe Unsubscribe" link at the bottom.
- Other mailings have a link to "update your email preferences," typically at the bottom.
- A last resort is to reply to the email and request to be taken off the sender's mailing list.
- If you unsubscribe from a mailing list but it doesn't work (i.e., you keep getting emails from that sender), you can designate the sender as a "blocked" sender so the email will at least go to your junk mail and not clog up your inbox.
- Periodically go through your junk-mail folder and see if there is anything in there you can unsubscribe from.

After unsubscribing on a regular basis, you should see a definite decrease in the number of emails coming in. You will love it.

Real-Life Example

Following a webinar I presented on email management, an attendee wrote that she was busy unsubscribing from numerous emails. The most incriminating one was Abercrombie Kids. Why incriminating? Her twins were now eighteen years old and way past fitting into Abercrombie Kids clothing. Better late than never!

2. Divert

There are probably many emails coming into your inbox that you want to continue to receive, but you don't need to see them the minute they arrive. Instead, you can divert them to subfolders so that they don't distract you from your important work and so you can read them at your leisure. Examples of such emails are:

- newsletters
- Linkedin and Facebook notitifcations
- sales ads from specific stores

Nearly every email program or manager lets you set up some form of **automated message filtering** to automatically forward the incoming email to a subfolder, thus bypassing your inbox. This is as simple as using folders to separate important mail from the clutter, based on sender, subject, or other variables.

Identify email that you don't need to see the minute it comes in and determine where it would make sense to route these pieces. For example, monthly newsletters could be routed to a folder labeled "To Read" (or if it is more helpful, use the newsletter's title in the folder name). Store sale ads can be routed to a folder labeled "Shopping." You can create as many folders and subfolders as you need, so set up a system that works best for you. Start simple and add as you need to.

NOTE: Most email programs give you the option to apply a filter or rule to the mail currently residing in your inbox, not just to future incoming email.

The bottom line is that in the future fewer emails will be arriving in your inbox to interrupt you and distract you from your goals. This is a proactive vs. reactive idea: you will read these emails when you say so, not when the sender says so.

Real-Life Example

My ninety-two-year-old Uncle Marvin lives out of town, so I don't see him very often, but he is prolific in sending me jokes and cartoons. I'm thrilled to get them since that lets me know that he is alive and well and enjoying himself, but I certainly don't need to read them when they arrive. So I route them to an "Uncle Marvin" folder and when I need a laugh, I know where to go.

3. Delete

It is time to get chummy with your DELETE button. In fact, it may become your best friend going forward.

How many emails come in that you need to see when they come in, but can be quickly read, need no action, and can be deleted? Yet, so many of us say to ourselves: **What if I might need this someday?** Instead, I suggest that you ask a different question: **What is the worst possible thing that could happen if I delete this email?**

I dare say that nine times out of ten, you can get the information again if you really need it at a later date, and you are much better off removing the clutter from your inbox than saving it for that "I-might-need-it-in-the-future" reason. Remember, focus on "quality vs. quantity."

<u>Helpful Shortcut</u>: When you are initially de-cluttering your inbox, a great shortcut to use when deleting email is to sort your inbox by sender or subject. This way, all of the emails from one sender or on a particular subject are grouped together for easy viewing and deleting. How gratifying it is to delete a group of thirty emails at once versus doing them one by one.

Real-Life Example

I worked with Barbara to regain control of her email inbox. Together we deleted large groups of emails, totaling 1,352 emails in just one session. She exclaimed to me at the end of the work session "I feel like I've lost weight without going on a diet." Deleting is very satisfying, and think of how many emails you are removing from your world that won't distract you from your priorities going forward.

Most importantly, when I checked in with Barbara a few months later, she had not one regret about having deleted any of the emails and she had kept up the good habits. She had "kept the weight off."

PSSST . . . maybe I shouldn't mention this, but deleted emails typically don't go away until you empty the trash, so if you don't empty the trash you have that safety valve as an insurance policy in case you should need it at a later date.

4. File

For items that you need to save for future reference, file them in folders.

A whole other book could be written about the details of a good filing system, so I will just touch upon some basic ideas here (See Sample File Structures on pages 31–34.)

- Keep your file structure simple and use just a few categories to start with. (A natural division at the highest level is business vs. personal.)
- Keep the folders you use for diverting email grouped together so that you know where to go to check the emails that automatically get filed (vs. the emails you manually file).
- Control the number of folders you create to one screen's worth so you don't have to scroll up and down to find the one you are looking for.

- When trying to figure out where to file an email, don't think about where to file it, but rather where you will think to look for it later (e.g., would you think of looking for a particular newsletter issue by the newsletter's name or the topic of the newsletter?).
- Never label a file "Miscellaneous." Using that label essentially allows you to put off making a decision.
- If over time a folder becomes too full and you can no longer find what you are looking for, consider creating subfolders within that folder.

Helpful Hint: You can always use a search function to find an email if for some reason you can't find it when you are looking for it in your new folder structure.

Helpful Habit: Don't think that you need to file a document each time you identify something to file. Instead put it in a "To File" folder and then periodically have a filing session. It is much more efficient to handle a batch of filing than to stop and file each time you have one thing to file.

Real-Life Example

Ellen co-owns a company with her husband and had been scrambling to stay on top of her email inbox. She was afraid to move emails out of her inbox because she thought she'd lose track of things, which made her anxious. Once we set up a simple file structure, created a subfolder "To File," and she set aside the time each week to file her emails, she felt relieved and more confident. By also fine-tuning her paper files and digital document files to be in line with the email file structure, she further streamlined her filing efforts and totally boosted her confidence in her overall file-maintenance efforts.

Figure 1: Sample File Structures

SAMPLE #1: Business and Personal

Inbox
    Business
        Action
            To Read
            Special Projects
            Tickler
            To File
        Clients
            Current
            Past
        Administration
        Marketing
        Networking

Personal
        Action
            To Read
            Bills to Pay
            Tickler
            To File
        Finances
            Tax-Related
        Family-Related
            Susan
            Tom

SAMPLE #2: Personal Only

Inbox
    Administration
        Finances
        House
        Taxes
        Entertainment
        Restaurants
        Travel
        Vacation
    Family
        Susan
        Tom
        Jan
        Mark
    Friends
    Tickler
        To Read
        To File

SAMPLE #3: Business Only

Inbox
    _Tickler*
    _To Read*
    _To File
Admin
Clients
    Company A
    Company B
    Company C
Financial
    Budgets
    Sales Projections
Marketing
Personal
Personnel
    Smith, John
    Jones, Susan
Projects
    Project A
    Project B
Training
Z-Reference*

* <u>Advanced Filing Concept Illustrated in Sample #3:</u>

Since the computer will automatically sort your folders alphabetically, you can force certain folders to sort to the top or bottom as you want. For example, put a special character "_","*", or "-" before a folder name and it sorts to the top. Add a "Z_" before a folder name and it will sort to the bottom. You can be creative in making the system work for you and locating folders in optimal places.

5. Act

After following steps 1–4, all that should be left in your inbox are items that you need to act on. So now what?

Your goal with the remaining emails is to take care of them and remove them from your inbox as soon as possible. Why? Compare your email inbox with the inbox on your desk. Which is more appealing, an overflowing box or one with just a few items in it? Of course the inbox with just a few items in it is more appealing. So you need to manage the remaining emails in our email inbox to avoid getting out of control again.

- For emails that you can take care of in one to two minutes, go ahead and take care of them. This might involve responding quickly, forwarding the email to someone else, or taking some other action. And if you can delete these emails when you are done acting on them, delete them. If they need to be filed, file them (or put them in the "To File" folder for filing later).

- For emails that require more than one to two minutes to handle, schedule time to work on them, but leave them in your inbox as a reminder that they need your attention.

Helpful Hint: If you are concerned that a long email response will lead to a drawn-out email conversation, pick up the phone to take care of business.

Tips on responding to emails:

1. Use a meaningful subject. The subject should communicate to the recipient what your email is about and what action you might be asking him or her to take.
2. Write concisely. Say what you mean, be clear, and use as few words as possible. This will save time for you and be easier for the recipient to read and respond to.

If you find that an email sits in your inbox for more than a week, re-evaluate it. Why is it still there? Is it really something that you are going to act on and that is important or is it "something that you might get around to someday, maybe"?

Real-Life Example

Martin had an overflowing email inbox which weighed him down and overwhelmed him, and as a result, he was stuck and his confidence was deflated. After he got his email inbox under control he felt so much lighter and productive. NOTE: being in motion boosts your confidence. You feel better and more in control when you take action.

ACTION ITEM:

Enter how many emails you started with in your inbox (from page 20) _____

How many emails are in your box after you applied the five steps? _____

You deleted and/or filed _____ (number of) emails. Celebrate your progress. That's fantastic progress. Keep it up.

Figure 2: Flow Charts for De-cluttering Your Inbox

Pass 1: Unsubscribe, Delete, and Divert

In this pass, you unsubscribe to email subscriptions, delete unnecessary email, and set up rules/filters to divert future emails as appropriate.

Pass 2: File

In this pass, you file emails that don't need action, but you need for future reference.

Pass 3: Act

In this pass, you act on the emails that need your attention and then file if appropriate.

Pass 1: Unsubscribe, Delete, and Divert

Email

Optional: Sort inbox by sender/subject to group like emails together

Is this a subscription? — **No** → Is this junk? — **No** → Leave in inbox (you will look at in **Pass 2**)

Yes ↓

Is this junk? — **Yes** →

Do you want to keep this subscription? — **No** → Unsubscribe → Delete all other emails associated with that subscription and/or sender

Pro Tip: Block sender so future emails go to junk folder

Yes ↓

Do you need to see this email right away? — **No** → Divert to a subfolder (set up rules/filters)

Pro Tip: Only keep the last 3 emails from this sender

Yes ↓

Leave in inbox (you will look at in **Pass 2**)

Pass 2: File

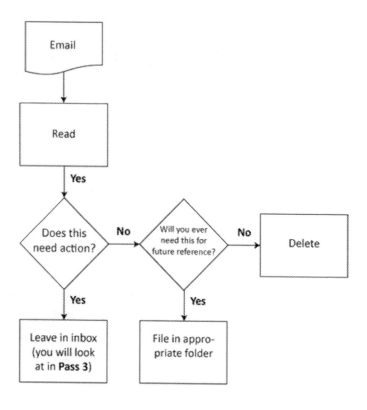

Pass 3: Act

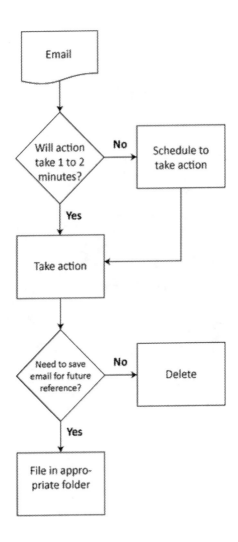

CHAPTER FIVE

Managing Your Email on a Daily Basis

Now that you have de-cluttered your email inbox and only have emails there that are current or need to be there, apply the same five steps to your email on a daily basis.

1. Unsubscribe
2. Divert (create rule/alert to route to a folder)
3. Delete
4. File
5. Act

Remember to periodically check the file folders that you divert emails to so that you don't overlook something that bypassed your inbox when it originally arrived.

To help you visualize the big picture of what you will be doing, I've included flow charts for Daily Email Management. (See page 46.)

Real-Life Example

Crystal developed a habit that worked well for her in starting her daily email-management effort. She does a first pass of her inbox to delete as many emails as possible. It is her way to warm up in the morning and have a good sense of progress from the start.

Recently, when she came back from a four-day vacation, this habit came in handy and she was able to quickly catch up on her email, unlike in the past when she would be so overwhelmed coming back from vacation that she dreaded her first day back dealing with email. What great progress. Go, Crystal!

Figure 3: Flow Charts for Daily Email Management

Pass 1: Unsubscribe, Delete, and Divert

In this pass, you unsubscribe to email subscriptions, delete unnecessary email, and set up rules/filters to divert future emails as appropriate.

Pass 2: Act and File

In this pass, you act on the emails that need your attention and then file if appropriate.

Pass 1: Unsubscribe, Delete, and Divert

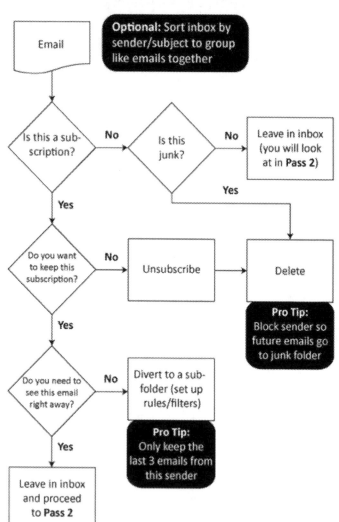

Pass 2: Act and File

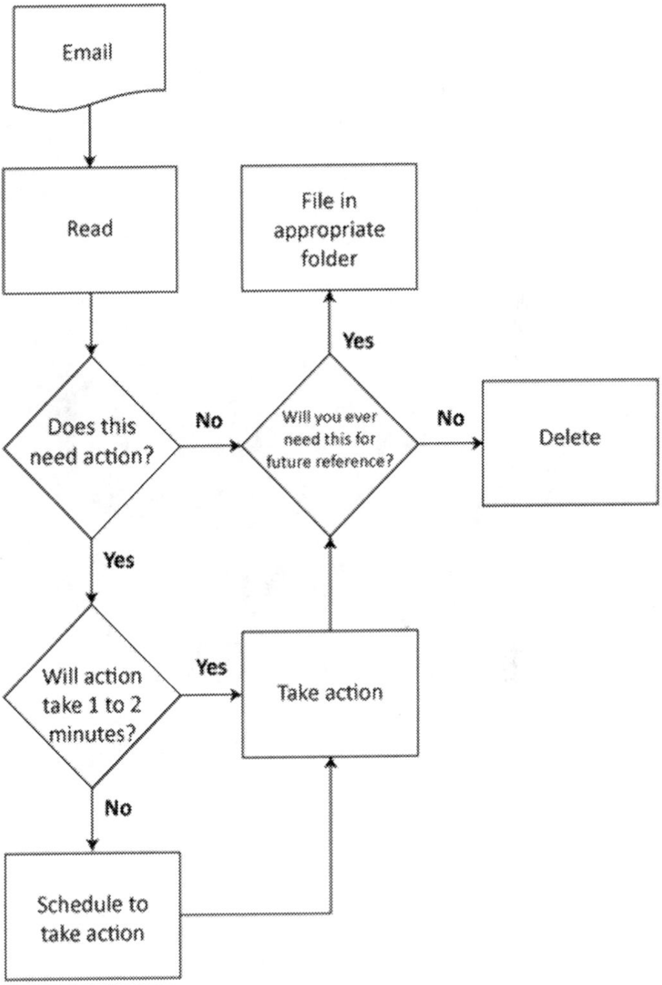

Email

Read

File in
appropriate
folder

Does this
need action? → No → Will you ever need this for future reference? → No → Delete

Yes (up to File in appropriate folder)

Yes (down)

Will action
take 1 to 2
minutes? → Yes → Take action

No

Schedule to
take action

DO YOU
WANT A PHD
IN EMAIL
MANAGEMENT?

CHAPTER SIX

Email Management 201

Below are a few advanced tips for when you are ready for some more sophisticated ideas to help you manage your email inbox.

Managing Different Email Addresses

The following strategies work particularly well when you are using an email-management platform such as Outlook or Thunderbird, which allows you to consolidate all email addresses into one tool.

To help compartmentalize your incoming email, consider using different email addresses:

- If you host an event or throw a party and don't want RSVPs and details to clutter your inbox, consider creating an additional email address to use temporarily for the event or party.
- Use separate email addresses for business and personal purposes.

- Use one email address when you register on a website, make airline reservations, make a purchase online, etc. so that these kinds of communications don't clutter up your main inbox(es).

Send Less Email

Try not to use the "Reply All" option. Don't send copies of your emails to people who don't really need them. Ask yourself, "Will the person who receives this email of mine be glad to get it?" If the answer is, "not sure," think twice about sending it. By spending less time writing and sending emails, you will help other people to spend less time reading them.

More on Filing

Use one file-tree structure for all files (email, digital documents, and paper documents). This way you will have a single decision-making logic no matter what you are filing. Of course, each filing system will be populated slightly differently, but they will all have the same basic categories and organization.

CHAPTER SEVEN

Maintenance Habits Going Forward

It's time to take a look again at that vision you identified at the beginning of this book. To reach that vision and to maintain it, you need good habits. It is like housekeeping: not necessarily fun, but critical to your reaching your goal and staying there.

1. **Reduce the number of times you check your email.**

   It is estimated that, on average, people check their email seventy times a day. Can you believe that? Wow! By reducing the number of times you check your email and by scheduling specific times during a day to check (e.g., five to six times a day), you will:

   • be proactive vs. reactive and take charge of your time;

- waste less time being interrupted by each incoming email; and
- be fully focused on your email function when you do check it and therefore be more productive.

I think that checking email is sometimes used as an excuse to avoid doing something else that we'd rather not do. I also believe that we are addicted to checking email. Remember, we don't want to miss out on anything and we get a shot of dopamine each time something new comes in. But let's break that habit.

Real-Life Example

On several occasions, people have told me that they either mark mail that they have already read as "unread" so that they see it more readily or they flag it as "important." This is usually done when they check their email on the fly on their phone and they want to make sure that they see it when they get back to the office or get home and can focus on it. If they checked their email fewer times a day, they would most likely be able to read and process the email completely instead of having to flag it for a future reading.

ACTION ITEM:

If you don't believe that you check your email as much as seventy times a day (including on your computer, tablet, and/or phone), track it for one day. Just keep a scratch pad nearby and make a little tick mark each time you check your email (it is like keeping a food log when you are trying to develop healthier eating habits). You'll be amazed how many times you really do check your email.

How many times do you think you check your email each day? _____

How many times do you actually check your email each day? _____

How many times would you like to check your email each day? _____

2. Turn off notifications, especially the ones that make a sound.

To be more proactive, turn off notifications so that you aren't interrupted each time an incoming email arrives (and this goes for all of your devices).

Real-Life Example

I have a client Stan who divides his week up into different kinds of days. Some days are spent creating new material for his clients and some days are spent on administrative efforts. On the days that he is doing client work, Stan turns off the notifications so he isn't distracted from being in the zone and creating for his clients. On the days he is doing administrative work, he leaves the notifications on because he dislikes doing administrative stuff, so the periodic interruptions break the monotony. It is all about making choices that work for him and sticking to those choices.

3. **Set aside time each day/week for file maintenance (to unsubscribe, delete, review, and empty the "To File" folder).**

Just like we change the oil in our cars every 4,000 miles and take the garbage out and do the laundry once or twice a week, we need a regular habit of performing maintenance on our email. This includes unsubscribing to emails, deleting emails that we don't have to keep any longer, reviewing our file structure, etc.

Real-Life Example

I met a woman recently who schedules fifteen minutes every two weeks just to unsubscribe. She does it on Friday afternoons when she is mentally tired and wants to do something mindless, yet productive. She makes progress, the task is manageable, and this behavior is a solid habit to keep.

Helpful Hint: Doing tasks such as email housekeeping for a specified length of time, especially if you have something fun or rewarding planned afterward, can be a motivating factor. Set a timer for twenty minutes and play "beat the clock." See how many emails you can delete in twenty minutes. This way you won't get sucked into the effort for an endless amount of time and you will make slow and steady progress on your maintenance.

4. Build on existing habits.

Do you take your snail mail and stand over your recycling/shredding/garbage containers to sort your mail? I'm guessing that you do, and that is a great habit. Take that same idea and apply it to your email.

Do you pay your bills on a particular day of the month (1st, 15th, 30th)? Consider scheduling your email-maintenance efforts at the same time so you knock two not-so-fun efforts off your to-do list. This may work especially well since you are most likely sitting at your desk already when you pay your bills.

5. Focus on single tasking vs. multitasking.

The allure of multitasking is thinking that we are getting more things done than if we did one thing at a time. The truth of the matter is that you can only physically focus on one thing at a time, so you end up starting and stopping tasks when you are multitasking and, of course, that is very inefficient. It has been shown that each time you are interrupted it takes sixty-four seconds to get re-engaged with what you were doing before you were interrupted according to a research associate in the School of Psychology at Cardiff University in Wales (http://www.rodalenews.com/computer-alerts-and-productivity). So multitasking ends of wasting a lot of time.

So multitasking actually wastes a lot of time.

I also think that multitasking tends to lead us to start many things and finish nothing. You'll have a better sense of accomplishment if you start one thing and finish it before going on to the next.

6. Reality check.

Though we might wish that regaining control of our email inbox will be a onetime effort, it is not. A good friend of mine recently wrote the following after implementing some of my tips.

> *I'm coming to terms with the fact that establishing and maintaining order is an ongoing effort. Celebrating small successes is an essential part of the process for me.*

This was a great revelation. Just like housekeeping, laundry, and cooking meals, being organized is an ongoing effort and the more you stick with your maintenance habits, the better success you will achieve and the larger positive impact you will make on your life. And don't forget to celebrate your progress each step of the way. Whether it is a pat on the back, doing a happy dance, or treating yourself with a reward, recognize your efforts and cheer yourself on.

Real-Life Example

I'll be the case study for this example since I'm human too. As my business has grown and the layers of complexity have piled on, I have been tempted to have multiple software programs open on my computer so that I can manage more in a day. (I have two screens to help with that functionality.) I have noticed that my stress level goes up and my sense of accomplishment goes down when I do this. So I have recommitted to focusing on one thing at a time, and lo and behold, my stress level has gone down and my sense of accomplishment and excitement about what I'm doing has gone up! I love it!

CONCLUSION

I have talked about:

- How we got to having unmanageable email inboxes
- Your personal vision
- Implementing the five steps to de-cluttering your email inbox and managing it on a daily basis
- Developing new habits going forward

Next Steps

To achieve the progress you are hoping for, it is helpful to add one or both of the following ingredients:

- Set goals that are quantifiable and realistic.
  Example: One screen's worth of emails in your inbox by a specific date. (Deadlines are motivating and keep you accountable.)
- Accountability.
  Example: Tell somebody you're on this path; buddy-up with somebody who wants to achieve the same goals.

If you need further professional assistance, you can hire me. I can work in-person if you live in the Chicago area or I can work virtually if you live farther away. Here's what I can do for you:

- Create a custom file structure for you.
- Further customize your specific email environment.
- Show you how to use filters/rules to divert email in your email platform.
- Provide accountability.
- Make de-cluttering your inbox and managing it in the future a fun and less dreadful task.

Final Thoughts

You have made it. You have gone through all of the material I wanted to share with you and hopefully you are revved up and ready to tackle your email inbox challenges. Consider yourself already on the path to success and freedom from your cluttered email inbox. And once you regain control of your inbox, you will be amazed at how that achievement will spill over into other areas of your life. There is no stopping you now.

A favorite quote of mine is, "Change happens, transformation is intentional." This quote resonates with me because while there is a lot beyond our control in our world (like email coming at us fast and furious), there is also a lot that is within our control. It is through dealing with what is within our control that we create transformation.

It is all about being intentional. Take charge of your email inbox and see how your life transforms.

Just when I thought I was finished writing this book, my editor (who also happens to be my sister Judy) relayed the following story to me. She and her ten-year-old grandson were parallel playing in her home office (i.e., he was doing a puzzle and she was doing some computer work). At one point her grandson looked over at her while she was checking her email and exclaimed with awe in his voice, "You have so few emails in your inbox." A sign of the times when a ten-year-old thinks an uncluttered inbox is unusual!

—— ACKNOWLEDGMENTS ——

I would like to thank my dear sister, Judy Gordon, for her collaboration and expert editing efforts. It was a thrill to see her work her magic on my words.

I would like to thank my daughter, Natalie Shay, for her encouragement, collaboration, and expertly designed flow charts.

I would like to thank my daughter, Gabriella Shay, for her collaboration on the cover design. Though I went a different direction, I want to share Gabriella's humorous idea for my cover design with you. When I told her my book title and asked for suggestions for the cover illustration, without hesitation she said "put a man holding a letter E." Silly me didn't get her joke. "It's an E-male, Mom." Thank you, Gabi.

And a global thank-you to all of my friends, family, and colleagues for their support and encouragement of my professional endeavors.

—— ABOUT THE AUTHOR ——

Bonnie Shay is a Professional Organizer and founder of Mariposa Creative Solutions. When she was a little girl, her idea of fun was to organize her family's kitchen pantry, cabinets, and drawers. She discovered many years later that it wasn't every kid's idea of a good time. Who knew?

But it planted the seed of an idea that underlies Mariposa Creative Solutions: that each of us loves and excels at different things and if we recognize that and do what we do best, we can make a difference in other people's lives and they can make a difference in ours.

And if you're reading this book, Bonnie's guess is that you are not like her—a person whose passion is to make order. But that is not something to feel bad about. Instead, recognize what you are good at, what you enjoy, and how to relieve that which weighs on you and keeps you from doing what you're good at and enjoy.

Wherever Bonnie goes, she aims to make order out of disorder, whatever shape it takes. She gets her clients unstuck and back to doing what they want to be doing in life. Besides email management, Bonnie specializes in residential organizing (any room or area in the house) and photo organizing (printed and digital photos).

Bonnie is a member of NAPO (The National Association of Professional Organizers) and on the board of NAPO-Chicago. She is also a certified Personal Photo Organizer and a member of APPO (The Association of Personal Photo Organizers).

She has been featured in several publications and enjoys presenting on a variety of organizing topics for live audiences, and on teleseminars and webinars.

Bonnie has a bachelor's degree from the College of Business at the University of Illinois, Urbana-Champaign.

For more than thirty years in the business world, Bonnie has developed systems, processes, and more efficient ways of doing a wide variety of functions including best business practices for small, medium, and large organizations.

Email: Bonnie@MariposaCreativeSolutions.com

Website: www.MariposaCreativeSolutions.com